SCHOLASTIC

Learning Express

English

Grammar and Writing

This book belongs to

_____

© 2013 Scholastic Education International (Singapore) Private Limited
A division of Scholastic Inc.

Previously published as Reading & Math Jumbo Workbook Grade 3 and 4, Summer Express 2-3 and
Summer Express 3-4 by Scholastic Inc.

For information regarding permission, write to:
Scholastic Education International (Singapore) Pte Ltd
81 Ubi Avenue 4, #02-28 UB.ONE, Singapore 408830
Email: education@scholastic.com.sg

For sales enquiries write to:

Latin America, Caribbean, Europe (except UK), Middle East and Africa
Scholastic International
557 Broadway, New York, NY 10012, USA
Email: intlschool@scholastic.com

Philippines
Scholastic Philippines
Penthouse 1, Prestige Tower, F. Ortigas Jr. Road,
Ortigas Center, Pasig City 1605
Email: educteam@scholastic.com.ph

Asia (excluding India and Philippines)
Scholastic Asia
Plaza First Nationwide, 161, Jalan Tun H S Lee,
50000 Kuala Lumpur, Wilayah Persekutuan Kuala Lumpur, Malaysia
Email: international@scholastic.com

Rest of the World
Scholastic Education International (Singapore) Pte Ltd
81 Ubi Avenue 4 #02-28 UB.ONE Singapore 408830
Email: education@scholastic.com.sg

Australia
Scholastic Australia Pty Ltd
PO Box 579, Gosford, NSW 2250
Email: scholastic_education@scholastic.com.au

New Zealand
Scholastic New Zealand Ltd
Private Bag 94407, Botany, Auckland 2163
Email: orders@scholastic.co.nz

India
Scholastic India Pvt. Ltd.
A-27, Ground Floor, Bharti Sigma Centre,
Infocity-1, Sector 34, Gurgaon (Haryana) 122001, India
Email: education@scholastic.co.in

Visit our website: www.scholastic.com.sg

First edition 2013
Reprinted 2013, 2018

ISBN 978-981-07-1369-0

Welcome to Scholastic Learning Express!

Helping your child build essential skills is easy!

These teacher-approved activities have been specially developed to make learning both accessible and enjoyable. On each page, you'll find:

Focus skill
The focus of each activity page is clearly indicated.

Meaningful learning
Each activity has been carefully designed to make your child's learning meaningful and fun.

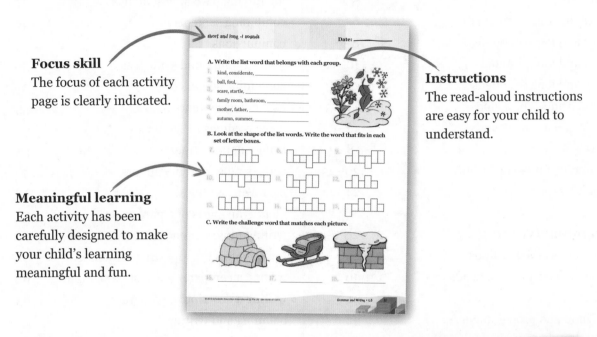

Instructions
The read-aloud instructions are easy for your child to understand.

This book also contains:

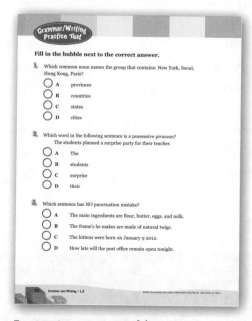

Instant assessment to ensure your child really masters the skills.

Completion certificate to celebrate your child's leap in learning.

Motivational stickers to mark the milestones of your child's learning path.

Contents

Spelling 5
short and long -a sounds 6–7
short and long -e sounds 8–9
short and long -i sounds 10–11
short and long -o sounds 12–13
short -u and /oo/ sounds 14–15
-er, -est, -ed, -ing sounds 16–17
plurals 18–19
commonly misspelled words 20–23
Spelling Practice Test 24–27

Grammar/Writing 28
statements and questions 29
exclamations and commands 30
nouns 31
common and proper nouns 32
using a and an 33
personal pronouns 34
subject and object pronouns 35
pronouns 36
prepositions 37
verbs 38
linking and helping verbs 39
adjectives 40–42
possessive adjectives 43
adjectives that compare 44–45
adverbs 46

identifying parts of a sentence 47
combining sentences 48
conjunctions 49
writing compound sentences 50
combining sentences 51–52
expanding sentences 53
using commas in sentences 54
using quotation marks 55
using similes and metaphors 56–57
narrowing a topic 58
identifying parts of a paragraph 59
writing topic sentences 60
topic sentence/supporting sentences ... 61
writing a compare/contrast paragraph ... 62
writing a descriptive paragraph 63
planning and writing
a persuasive paragraph 64
keeping a journal 65
finding errors 66
proofreading 67–68
fixing run-on sentences 69
Grammar/Writing Practice Test 70–74

Answer Key 75–78
Certificate 79
Stickers 81

Spelling

In this section your child reviews the spelling of long and short vowels. He or she will also be introduced to plural forms and commonly misspelled words.

What To Do

Have your child complete the activity pages. Review your child's answers. Remember, answers to the activities are in the back of the book if you need them.

Keep On Going!

Play a spelling game with your child. Say:
I am thinking of a word.

> It begins with the hard -*g* sound.
> It has a long -*a* vowel.
> It ends with a *t* sound.
> It has a silent *e* at the end.
> Say the word and spell it. [gate]

Take turns giving and receiving clues.

Date: _____

 *The **short -a** sound is often spelled with the letter **a**.*
*The **long -a** sound can be spelled with the letters **a_e**, **ai** or **ay**.*

A. Read and write each word. Then organize the list words by the spelling of their a sound.

📝 List Words

1. dragon _____
2. today _____
3. brave _____
4. plains _____
5. mistake _____
6. raise _____
7. maybe _____
8. gather _____
9. wait _____
10. holiday _____
11. handle _____
12. became _____

short -a	ai
_____	_____
_____	_____
_____	_____

a_e	ay
_____	_____
_____	_____
_____	_____

🏆 Challenge Words

13. parade _____
14. costume _____
15. balloons _____

B. Write four list words that have three vowels (not including y).

_____   _____   _____   _____

© 2013 Scholastic Education International (S) Pte Ltd   ISBN 978-981-07-1369-0

A. Proofread the letter. Circle the six misspelled words. Write them correctly on the lines below.

Dear Chelsey,

    Chinese New Year is almost here! It is celebrated in January or February. The date of the holliday depends on the movement of the moon. The children in my family wate all year to receive red paper envelopes full of money from our family and friends. My favorite part of the celebration is the parade. This year my braive brother will wear the dragin costume with some of his friends. They will gether in the streets and entertain the crowds. Maybee one day you can visit during this wonderful celebration.

Your friend,

Mia

_____ _____ _____

_____ _____ _____

B. Write the list word for each definition. The shaded boxes will answer the riddle.

Where do dragons go to dance?

1. an error
2. to lift
3. to come together
4. the past tense of **become**
5. the present time
6. open rolling land
7. part that can be grabbed to help move something

*The **short -e** sound is often spelled with the letter **e**.*
*The **long -e** sound can be spelled with the letters **ea** or **ee**.*

A. Read and write each word. Then organize the list words by the spelling of their e sound.

List Words

				short -e	ea
1.	scream	_____			
2.	cheek	_____			
3.	member	_____			
4.	freeze	_____			
5.	next	_____			
6.	reason	_____			
7.	asleep	_____	**ee**		
8.	check	_____			
9.	team	_____			
10.	enter	_____			
11.	between	_____			
12.	reach	_____			

Challenge Words

13.	basketball	_____
14.	soccer	_____
15.	tennis	_____

B. Write four list words that begin with more than one consonant.

_____ _____ _____ _____

A. Use a list word to complete each analogy.

1. **Push** is to **pull** as **exit** is to _____.

2. **Sing** is to **joyful** as _____ is to **scared**.

3. **Puddle** is to **melt** as **ice** is to _____.

4. **Teacher** is to **class** as **coach** is to _____.

5. **Sister** is to **family** as _____ is to **group**.

6. **Narrow** is to **wide** as _____ is to **awake**.

B. Circle each of the list words hidden in the puzzle. The words go across, down, backward and diagonally. Write each word in the correct group.

r	k	c	e	h	c	n	o	d	g	m
b	a	r	i	s	c	r	e	a	m	e
e	r	r	f	g	r	a	b	x	y	n
t	a	e	s	r	m	a	e	t	t	t
w	h	a	a	s	e	a	n	d	a	e
e	d	c	i	s	m	e	m	b	e	r
e	s	h	x	c	o	t	z	t	l	i
n	c	h	e	e	k	n	l	e	g	r
a	v	m	a	p	e	e	l	s	a	c

Across

_____

_____

_____

Backward

_____

_____

_____

Down

_____

_____

_____

Diagonally

_____

_____

_____

C. Find a word in each sentence that could be replaced by a challenge word. Cross it out and write the challenge word on the line.

7. Mike kicked the big ball down the field and into the net. _____

8. Kayla won the chess match last Friday. _____

9. Sam grabbed the ball and shot it through the hoop. _____

The **short -i** sound is often spelled with the letter **i**.
The **long -i** sound can be spelled with the letters **i_e** or **igh**.

A. Read and write each word. Then organize the list words by the spelling of their i sound.

📝 List Words

		short -i	i_e
1.	winter _____		
2.	surprise _____		
3.	bright _____		
4.	middle _____		
5.	polite _____		
6.	frighten _____		
7.	children _____	**igh**	
8.	tight _____		
9.	while _____		
10.	strike _____		
11.	kitchen _____		
12.	slight _____		

🏆 Challenge Words

13. sleigh _____

14. igloo _____

15. icicle _____

B. Write any four list words that end in silent e.

_____   _____

© 2013 Scholastic Education International (S) Pte Ltd ISBN 978-981-07-1369-0

Date: _____

A. Write the list word that belongs with each group.

1. kind, considerate, _____
2. ball, foul, _____
3. scare, startle, _____
4. family room, bathroom, _____
5. mother, father, _____
6. autumn, summer, _____

B. Look at the shape of the list words. Write the word that fits in each set of letter boxes.

7.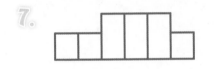

8.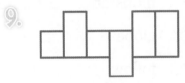

9.

10.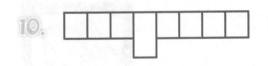

11.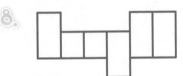

12.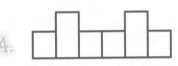

13.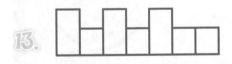

14.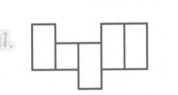

15.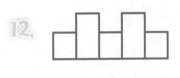

C. Write the challenge word that matches each picture.

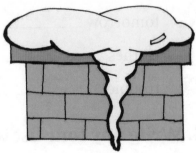

16. _____

17. _____

18. _____

Date: _____

 *The **short -o** sound is often spelled with the letter **o**.*
*The **long -o** sound can be spelled with the letters*
o_e or ow.

A. Read and write each word. Then organize the list words by the spelling of their o sound.

List Words

	short -o	o_e
1. pillow _____	_____	_____
2. rocket _____	_____	_____
3. alone _____	_____	_____
4. below _____	_____	
5. monster _____		
6. globe _____	**ow**	
7. follow _____	_____	
8. holler _____	_____	
9. whole _____	_____	
10. window _____		
11. bottle _____	**short -o and ow**	
12. suppose _____	_____	

Challenge Words

13. tomorrow _____

14. clothes _____

15. trouble _____

B. Write any four list words that have double consonants.

_____   _____   _____   _____

© 2013 Scholastic Education International (S) Pte Ltd ISBN 978-981-07-1369-0

A. Use list words to complete the story.

Pillow fights are the greatest! The best pillow fight I ever had was with my brother. He

threw his _____ so hard that it flew over my head like a _____

into space. Seconds later, I heard my mom _____, "Stop throwing the pillows.

One may fly out the _____!" I couldn't resist. I blasted my pillow toward my

brother. I missed my aim and it broke a _____ _____ of my mom's

perfume. I don't _____ we'll have any more pillow fights around here!

B. Complete the crossword puzzle using the list word that fits each clue.

Across

3. complete
8. rhymes with **hollow**
9. spaceship
10. a noun you can look through
11. antonym for **together**
12. a scary creature

Down

1. the world
2. antonym for **above**
4. to shout
5. a soft place for your head
6. a glass container
7. rhymes with **grows**

C. Write the challenge words in alphabetical order.

1. _____ 2. _____ 3. _____

Date: _____

The **short -u** sound is often spelled with the letter **u**.
The **/oo/** sound can be spelled with the letters **u**, **oo** or **ou**.

A. Read and write each word. Then organize the list words by the spelling of their u sound.

List Words

		short **-u**	long **-u**
1.	super	_____	_____	_____
2.	coupon	_____	_____	_____
3.	until	_____	_____	_____
4.	loose	_____		
5.	ruler	_____	**oo**	**ou**
6.	group	_____	_____	_____
7.	shampoo	_____	_____	_____
8.	number	_____	_____	_____
9.	soup	_____		
10.	sudden	_____		
11.	duty	_____		
12.	caboose	_____		

Challenge Words

13.	groceries	_____
14.	teaspoon	_____
15.	supermarket	_____

B. A noun is a word that names a person, place or thing. Write any four list words that are nouns.

_____   _____   _____   _____

Date: _____

A. Write the list word that completes each sentence in the puzzle. Then write the letters in the shaded boxes in order to spell the name of a grocery item.

1. Mom used a _____ to save a dollar on the price of a ticket.

2. Molly's _____ showed that her plant had grown three inches.

3. A _____ of fish is called a school.

4. Spot's collar was too _____, and he squirmed out of it.

5. Always _____ your hair after swimming.

6. The beach party was great fun _____ it started raining.

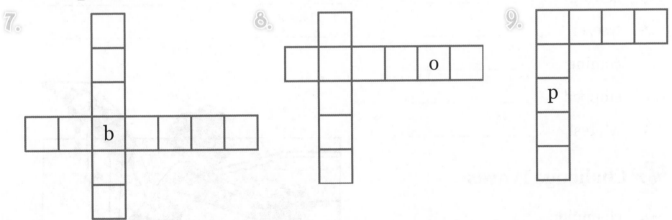

_ _ _ _ _ _ _

B. Write two list words that share a common letter to complete each puzzle.

7.

8.   o

9.   p

b

C. Guide words are listed at the top of each page in a dictionary. They show the first and last words found on that page. Write each challenge word on the dictionary page where it would be found.

sunset • supply

_____

grizzly • grouch

_____

team • temper

_____

Date: _____

 When a word ends with one vowel and one consonant (VC), double the consonant before adding an ending. *Example:* run *becomes* running. *When a word ends with a silent* e, *the* e *is dropped before adding an ending. Example:* rake *becomes* raking.

A. Read and write each word. Then organize the list words by their endings.

📝 List Words

			-er ending	**-est** ending
1.	swimmer	_____	_____	_____
2.	wisest	_____	_____	_____
3.	hoped	_____	_____	_____
4.	shopping	_____		
5.	clapped	_____		
6.	safer	_____	**-ed** ending	**-ing** ending
7.	biggest	_____	_____	_____
8.	getting	_____	_____	_____
9.	freezer	_____	_____	_____
10.	coming	_____		
11.	stopped	_____		
12.	whitest	_____		

🏆 Challenge Words

13. champion _____
14. medal _____
15. compete _____

B. Write four list words that have long vowel sounds.

_____   _____   _____   _____

© 2013 Scholastic Education International (S) Pte Ltd ISBN 978-981-07-1369-0

Date: _____

A. Read each base word and write its matching list word with an ending. Then check the rule that applies to each word.

	Base Word	List Word	Double the final consonant	Drop the silent e
1.	big			
2.	hope			
3.	come			
4.	get			
5.	white			
6.	wise			

B. Write a list word to complete each sentence. The shaded boxes will answer the riddle.

What did the sneezing champion win at the Olympics?

1. Are you _____ over today?

2. We are _____ for new shoes.

3. We _____ at the end of the show.

4. Our bus _____ at the corner.

5. My best friend is a strong _____.

6. Let's get ice cream from the _____.

7. I _____ my mother would agree.

8. Riding a bike is _____ with a helmet.

Date: _____

 There are different ways to form the plurals of words. To form the plural of most words ending in **f** *or* **fe**, *change the* **f** *or* **fe** *to* **v** *and add* **-es**. *Example:* leaf, leaves. *Some words have unusual plural forms. Example:* man, men.

A. Read and write each word. Then organize the list words by the way the plurals are formed.

List Words

1. loaves   _____
2. geese   _____
3. wolves   _____
4. calves   _____
5. oxen   _____
6. children   _____
7. halves   _____
8. teeth   _____
9. thieves   _____
10. scarves   _____
11. cacti   _____
12. mice   _____
13. knives   _____
14. women   _____
15. shelves   _____

changes -f to -ves

_____   _____

_____   _____

_____   _____

_____   _____

changes -oo- to -ee-

_____   _____

unusual plural forms

_____   _____

_____   _____

_____

Challenge Words

16. reptiles   _____
17. tortoises   _____
18. alligator   _____
19. predators   _____
20. vertebrates   _____

    © 2013 Scholastic Education International (S) Pte Ltd ISBN 978-981-07-1369-0

Date: _____

A. Write the plural list word in the puzzle for each singular form below. Then write the letters in the shaded boxes in order on the blanks below to complete the fact.

1.	calf	2.	goose	3.	half
4.	tooth	5.	shelf	6.	cactus
7.	ox	8.	knife	9.	thief
10.	scarf	11.	woman	12.	mouse
13.	loaf	14.	child	15.	wolf

16. ___ ___ ___ ___ ___ ___ can run across ceilings because their feet are like suction cups.

B. Correct the mistakes in the paragraph below. Then write the misspelled words correctly on the lines provided.

Reptils are cold-blooded vertebraetes. This means that their body temperatures stay about the same temperature as their surroundings. Alligaters, lizards, snakes and tortuises are examples of these scaly skinned animals.

Many reptiles are preddators, which means they hunt other animals for food.

_____   _____

_____   _____

_____

Date: _____

 Some words do not follow common spelling patterns. Their spellings must be memorized.

A. Read and write each word. Then write an idea that will help you memorize each spelling. For example, *been* has two *e*'s.

List Words

1. been _____ _____
2. other _____ _____
3. favorite _____ _____
4. does _____ _____
5. these _____ _____
6. before _____ _____
7. friend _____ _____
8. always _____ _____
9. their _____ _____
10. done _____ _____
11. people _____ _____
12. thought _____ _____

Challenge Words

13. mammal _____
14. canines _____
15. breed _____

B. Write four list words that will be the toughest to learn to spell.

_____ _____

© 2013 Scholastic Education International (S) Pte Ltd ISBN 978-981-07-1369-0

Date: _____

A. Write the list word that belongs in each group.

1. this, those, _____

2. finished, completed, _____

3. especially liked, preferred, _____

4. pal, comrade, _____

5. _____, during, after

6. _____, sometimes, never

7. his, her, our, _____

8. persons, humans, _____

B. Write a list word that fits in the letter boxes. Use a list word only once.

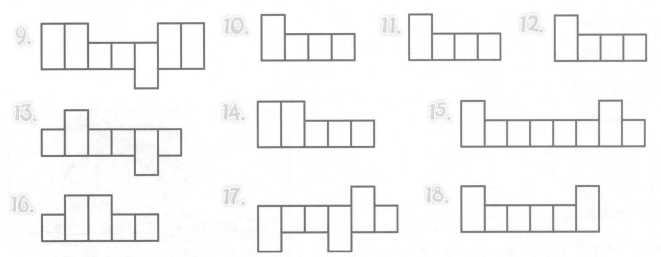

9. 10. 11. 12.

13. 14. 15.

16. 17. 18.

C. Find the word in the sentence that could be replaced by a challenge word. Cross it out and write the challenge word on the line.

19. The elephant is the largest living animal. _____

20. Labrador retrievers are an excellent kind of dog for families.

_____

21. Dogs are used to help guard, herd, track and hunt. _____

Date: _____

 Some words do not follow common sound-spelling patterns. The spellings of these words must be memorized.

A. Read and write each word. Then organize the list words by the number of vowels in them.

List Words

one vowel   two vowels

1. once   _____   _____   _____

2. forty   _____   _____   _____

3. meant   _____   _____

4. young   _____   **three vowels**   _____

5. island   _____   _____   _____

6. another   _____   _____   _____

7. truly   _____   _____   _____

8. against   _____   _____

9. beauty   _____   _____

10. toward   _____   _____

11. calendar   _____

12. answer   _____

13. often   _____

14. machine   _____

15. cousin   _____

Challenge Words

16. portrait   _____

17. sculpture   _____

18. artistic   _____

19. landscape   _____

20. masterpiece   _____

A. Write the list word that belongs with each group of words.

1. peninsula, mountain, _____

2. aunt, uncle, _____

3. twenty, sixty, _____

4. equipment, appliance, _____

5. pretty, handsome, _____

6. month, date, _____

B. Use proofreading marks to correct the 11 mistakes in the paragraph.

Wunce upon a time there was a yung boy who would not study. He ment to study, but
he always forgot. Thus, he would ofen need to guess an anser because he truely did not
know it. While walking tward his house after school, he decided to lean aginst a tree. He
watched a squirrel nibble on a nut. Anuther squirrel scampered up the tree. the squirrels
were so fascinating the boy decided to learn about them That night he discovered how
interesting it is to study.

C. Write the challenge word for each definition. Then use the picture code to answer the question below.

7. a statue ___ ___ ___ ___ ___ ___ ___ ___
              ☆

8. a picture of a land scene ___ ___ ___ ___ ___ ___ ___ ___
                                   ✳

9. something done with great skill ___ ___ ___ ___ ___ ___ ___ ___
                                    ✹   ✄
   ___ ___ ___

10. showing talent ___ ___ ___ ___ ___ ___ ___
                    ◎   ✷

11. a picture of someone ___ ___ ___ ___ ___ ___ ___
                             ✎   ✍

What is the most expensive painting in the world?

12. The "___ ___ ___ ___   ___ ___ ___ ___," painted by Leonardo da Vinci,
        ✹ ✎ ✳ ◎   ☆ ✄ ✷ ✍

is worth at least 100 million dollars.

Fill in the bubble next to the correct answer.

1. Which word does NOT have a **long -a** sound?

   ○ **A**   make

   ○ **B**   boat

   ○ **C**   bay

   ○ **D**   wait

2. Which word has the **short -a** sound?

   ○ **A**   bait

   ○ **B**   brave

   ○ **C**   handle

   ○ **D**   gray

3. Which word does NOT have the **long -e** sound?

   ○ **A**   between

   ○ **B**   reason

   ○ **C**   reach

   ○ **D**   check

© 2013 Scholastic Education International (S) Pte Ltd   ISBN 978-981-07-1369-0

Fill in the bubble next to the correct answer.

4. Which word does NOT have the **long -o** sound?

◯ **A**   whole

◯ **B**   suppose

◯ **C**   window

◯ **D**   bottle

5. Which word has a **long -i** sound?

◯ **A**   trouble

◯ **B**   middle

◯ **C**   while

◯ **D**   kitchen

6. Which word has the **long -u** sound?

◯ **A**   fur

◯ **B**   sudden

◯ **C**   youth

◯ **D**   full

Spelling Practice Test

Fill in the bubble next to the correct answer.

7. Which word is spelled correctly?

     ◯ **A**   shoping

     ◯ **B**   swimmer

     ◯ **C**   comeing

     ◯ **D**   bigest

8. Which word is misspelled?

     ◯ **A**   freezeer

     ◯ **B**   whitest

     ◯ **C**   stopped

     ◯ **D**   wisest

9. Which word is the correct plural form of **ox**?

     ◯ **A**   oxs

     ◯ **B**   oxes

     ◯ **C**   oxen

     ◯ **D**   ox

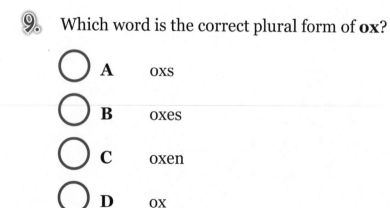

Spelling Practice Test

Fill in the bubble next to the correct answer.

10. Which word is spelled correctly?

     ◯ **A**   mammel

     ◯ **B**   uther

     ◯ **C**   breded

     ◯ **D**   canines

11. Which word is spelled correctly?

     ◯ **A**   befor

     ◯ **B**   peeple

     ◯ **C**   allways

     ◯ **D**   favorite

12. Which word is misspelled?

     ◯ **A**   geese

     ◯ **B**   cacti

     ◯ **C**   loafes

     ◯ **D**   knives

© 2013 Scholastic Education International (S) Pte Ltd ISBN 978-981-07-1369-0

Grammar/Writing

To be a successful writer, you have to understand the rules of the game. Grammar provides the rules your child needs to write clear and interesting selections in a variety of writing modes: expository, persuasive and narrative.

The activities in this section review the rules for good writing. Those rules include knowing parts of speech (nouns, pronouns, adjectives, verbs, adverbs) and how to use them to build clear, interesting and well-developed sentences and paragraphs.

What To Do

Each new skill starts with a definition or explanation. Have your child read the definitions or explanations on the activity page. Then have your child complete the activity. Review his or her work together. Let your child know that he or she is doing a great job!

Keep On Going!

Read your child's writing assignments. Prompt your child with suggestions such as: *Can you give a clearer explanation? How does that idea relate to the next idea? What is the main idea? Do you have details to support it? Why not compare the actions of the main characters?*

© 2013 Scholastic Education International (S) Pte Ltd ISBN 978-981-07-1369-0

Date: _____

 A **statement** is a sentence that tells something. It ends with a period.
A **question** is a sentence that asks something. It ends with a question mark.

A. Read each sentence. Write Q on the line if the sentence is a question. Write S if the sentence is a statement.

1. Where did the ant live? _____

2. The ant had many cousins. _____

3. She found the crumb under a leaf. _____

4. How will she carry it? _____

5. Who came along first? _____

6. The lizard wouldn't help. _____

7. He said he was too cold. _____

8. Why did the rooster fly away? _____

B. The sentences below do not make sense. Rewrite the words in the correct order.

1. How crumb did carry the ant the?

   _____

2. She herself it carried.

   _____

3. The busy rooster was very.

   _____

Date: _____

 *An **exclamation** is a sentence that shows strong feeling. It ends with an exclamation point. A **command** is a sentence that gives an order. It ends with a period.*

A. Read each sentence. Write E on the line if the sentence is an exclamation. Write C if the sentence is a command.

1. They chase buffaloes! _____

2. You have to go. _____

3. Wait at the airport. _____

4. It snows all the time! _____

5. Alligators live in the sewers! _____

6. Look at the horse. _____

7. That's a great-looking horse! _____

8. Write a letter to Seymour. _____

B. Complete each exclamation and command. The punctuation mark at the end of each line is a clue.

1. I feel _____!

2. Help your _____.

3. That's a _____!

4. I lost _____!

5. Turn the _____.

6. Come watch the _____.

7. Please let me _____.

© 2013 Scholastic Education International (S) Pte Ltd ISBN 978-981-07-1369-0

*A **noun** names a person, place, thing or idea.*

Fill in the letter beneath the word in each sentence that is a noun.

1. The world's first toothbrushes weren't brushes at all.
        (a)   (b)   (c)   (d)

2. They were pencil-sized twigs that were frayed at one end.
        (a)   (b) (c)   (d)

3. These "chew sticks" were found in many ancient Egyptian tombs!
        (a)   (b)   (c)   (d)

4. The oldest bristle toothbrush was made in China over 500 years ago.
     (a)   (b)   (c)   (d)

5. The stiff bristles came from the necks of hogs.
   (a)   (b)   (c)   (d)

6. They were attached to handles carved out of bone or bamboo.
        (a)   (b)   (c)   (d)

7. The early Chinese toothbrushes were known for having hard bristles.
      (a)   (b)   (c)   (d)

8. Europeans who brushed used softer toothbrushes made of horsehair.
     (a)   (b)   (c) (d)

9. But any natural animal hair could introduce germs to the mouth.
   (a)   (b)   (c)   (d)

10. In 1938, Americans could buy the very first nylon-bristled toothbrush.
    (a)   (b)   (c)   (d)

11. Nylon was a new fiber that was safer and cleaner to use.
       (a)   (b)   (c)   (d)

12. Today, you can get toothbrushes in any size, stiffness, shape and color.
       (a)   (b)   (c)   (d)

Date: _____

 A **proper noun** *names a particular person, place or thing.* A **common noun** *names any person, place or thing.*

Write a proper noun that is an example of each common noun. The first one has been done for you.

1. state   _____ Arizona _____
2. singer   _____
3. river   _____
4. artist   _____
5. woman   _____
6. mountain   _____
7. athlete   _____
8. game   _____
9. shampoo   _____
10. song   _____

Write a common noun to name the group that includes each proper noun. The first one has been done for you.

11. Brazil   _____ country _____
12. Harry Potter   _____
13. Taylor Swift   _____
14. Honda   _____
15. *Lord of the Rings*   _____
16. Tokyo   _____
17. Shakespeare   _____
18. April   _____
19. Tuesday   _____
20. Gandhi   _____

Date: _____

A *and* **an** *are* **articles**. *They are noun signals. They let you know a noun is coming up in a sentence.*

Use **a** *when the word following it begins with a consonant sound. Use* **an** *when the word following it begins with a vowel sound.*

Write the correct article in the blank.

1. There was _____ opening in the cave.

2. Michael hid in _____ hollow tree.

3. I looked under the water and saw _____ big red crab.

4. _____ umbrella was lying open on the floor.

5. Judy stood by _____ odd-looking structure.

6. Matthew was being followed by _____ animal.

7. The treasure was buried on _____ piece of property.

8. Joshua did _____ good trick with the cards.

9. Julie was sailing on _____ rickety old boat.

10. Peggy wants to be _____ pilot when she grows up.

11. Bigfoot was _____ friendly monster.

12. Ms Betty broke her crown when she fell down on _____ clown.

13. _____ apple a day will keep the doctor away.

14. The girls found three peas in _____ pod.

15. The girl took _____ order for the yearbook.

Date: _____

Personal pronouns *are words used in the place of nouns.*

> ### Example
> **Katie** went out to finish her chores and then **she** went out to play.
> "She" (pronoun) takes the place of "Katie" (proper noun).

Underline the personal pronouns listed below in the following sentences.

> I   me   you   he   him   she   her   it   we   us   they   them

1. Greg read the book and returned it to the library.

2. The teacher chose Lisa and me to hand out the papers.

3. You will represent the school at the spelling bee.

4. Did I receive a phone call?

5. Steven, please help him with the math homework.

6. All of us will be attending the football game.

7. Who will help them finish the decorations?

8. Tell her that she won the prize.

9. We will have to drive them to the party.

10. Please hang it up on the back wall.

11. How many of you will be able to attend?

12. Only four of us ate lunch in the cafeteria.

© 2013 Scholastic Education International (S) Pte Ltd ISBN 978-981-07-1369-0

Date: _____

 A **subject pronoun** — **I, you, he, she, it, they** *or* **we** — *can replace the subject of a sentence. An* **object pronoun** — **me, you, him, her, it, us** *or* **them** — *can replace a noun that is the object of an action verb or that follows a preposition.*

A. Choose the pronoun in brackets ( ) that completes each sentence and write it on the line. Then identify the kind of pronoun in the sentence by writing S for subject or O for object.

1. _____ took a boat trip through the Everglades. (We, Us)   _____

2. The boat's captain gave _____ a special tour. (we, us)   _____

3. The captain said, "_____ will love the wildlife here!" (You, Us)   _____

4. _____ brought an instant camera in my backpack. (I, Me)   _____

5. I used _____ to photograph birds, turtles and alligators. (he, it)   _____

6. My sister Kit carried paper and pencils with _____. (she, her)   _____

7. Kit used _____ to sketch scenes of the Everglades. (they, them)   _____

8. _____ is an excellent artist. (She, Her)   _____

B. Rewrite each sentence. Replace the underlined words with the correct subject or object pronoun.

1. Our grandparents sent a postcard to my sister, my brother and me.

   _____

2. The postcard was addressed to my older brother.

   _____

C. Write two sentences. In the first, use a subject pronoun. In the second, use an object pronoun.

1. _____

2. _____

© 2013 Scholastic Education International (S) Pte Ltd ISBN 978-981-07-1369-0

Circle the correct noun that matches the meaning of each underlined pronoun.

1. Checkers is a very old game; <u>it</u> was played in Egypt over 4,000 years ago!

   (a) board game   (c) checkers

   (b) Egypt   (d) years

2. Players then were neither children nor old folks; <u>they</u> were warriors and rulers.

   (a) players   (c) folks

   (b) children   (d) warriors

3. How do we know checkers was played in Egypt? <u>It</u> appears in ancient paintings.

   (a) ancient   (c) paintings

   (b) proof   (d) Egypt

4. "Enemy" pieces were "captured" by opponents <u>who</u> tried to defeat each other.

   (a) enemy   (c) opponents

   (b) pieces   (d) other

5. The oldest known book about checkers was published in Spain in 1547. <u>Its</u> author was Antonio Torquemada.

   (a) the book's   (c) the game's

   (b) the author's (d) Spain's

6. The world's largest checkerboard, <u>which</u> uses big round pillows for playing pieces, is in Mississippi.

   (a) pieces   (c) pillows

   (b) Mississippi   (d) checkerboard

© 2013 Scholastic Education International (S) Pte Ltd ISBN 978-981-07-1369-0

Prepositions *show the relationship between a noun or pronoun and another word or group of words in a sentence such as* **in, on, of, for, from** *or* **at**. *Groups of words introduced by a preposition are called* **prepositional phrases**.

A. Read each sentence. Underline each group of words that begins with a preposition, and circle the preposition. Some sentences have more than one prepositional phrase.

1. The boy cut out pictures of mountains, rivers and lakes.

2. He enjoyed pasting them on the walls of his room.

3. His father decided that he would take his son on a camping trip.

4. They carried supplies in a backpack and a knapsack.

5. The boy drank a hot drink from his father's mug.

6. That afternoon they hiked in the mountains for hours.

7. They found many campers at the Lost Lake.

8. The boy and his father continued on their journey.

9. Finally, they stopped at a quiet place for the night.

10. The boy and his father ate and slept in a tent.

11. The tent kept them safe from the wind and rain.

12. What else will they see on their camping trip?

B. Complete each sentence with a prepositional phrase.

1. Let's go to the store _____.

2. I just received a letter _____.

3. Eduardo found his missing sneaker _____.

4. Tanya always plays soccer _____.

Date: _____

 *A **verb** tells the action in a sentence.*

Fill in the letter beneath the word that is a verb.

1. Did you know that bats are the only mammals that can fly?
   - ⓐ   ⓑ   ⓒ   ⓓ

2. Many people fear bats, but bats are really very important to us.
   - ⓐ ⓑ   ⓒ   ⓓ

3. Bats eat half their body weight in bugs every night.
   - ⓐ   ⓑ ⓒ ⓓ

4. Most bats are harmless to humans and valuable to nature's balance.
   - ⓐ   ⓑ   ⓒ   ⓓ

5. Bat mothers generally produce only one baby each year.
   - ⓐ ⓑ ⓒ ⓓ

6. Bats usually live in caves or other dark places.
   - ⓐ ⓑ ⓒ ⓓ

7. Each year, vandals destroy thousands of bats by blocking cave entrances.
   - ⓐ ⓑ   ⓒ   ⓓ

8. Bats are not really blind, but people believe they are.
   - ⓐ ⓑ ⓒ ⓓ

9. As for the belief that bats carry rabies, this is untrue.
   - ⓐ   ⓑ   ⓒ   ⓓ

10. You're more likely to be hit by a falling star than to
    - ⓐ   ⓑ

    get rabies from a bat.
    - ⓒ ⓓ

Date: _____

 The most common linking and helping verb is **be.** *Am, is, are, was and* **were** *are forms of the verb.*

Circle the correct form of be for each sentence.

1. Last spring, my brother and I _____ helping Uncle Rusty, who is a rancher.

   (a) are   (c) were

   (b) was   (d) have been

2. The first day we got there — it _____ a Friday — one of his mares had a new foal.

   (a) has been   (c) may be

   (b) was   (d) was being

3. Just before the birth, the mother horse _____ quietly pacing in her stall.

   (a) had been   (c) were

   (b) has been   (d) would be

4. That was the first time I _____ so close to such a big newborn animal.

   (a) being   (c) were

   (b) have been   (d) had been

5. The newborn's wobbly legs _____ longer than its body, yet the baby stood right up.

   (a) are   (c) were

   (b) was   (d) have been

6. "That's the way it _____ with newborn foals," said Uncle Rusty with a smile.

   (a) should be   (c) might

   (b) have been   (d) were

7. "By summer, that foal _____ a frisky young horse racing its mom," he added.

   (a) was   (c) were

   (b) will be   (d) have been

8. We had such a great time on the ranch, Uncle Rusty predicted that we _____ back soon.

   (a) was   (c) were

   (b) would be   (d) have been

Date: _____

 Adjectives *describe or tell more about things.*

Fill in the letter beneath the word (s) in each sentence that is an adjective.

1. The world's tropical rain forests are amazing places.
          (a)   (b) (c) (d)

2. Rain forests get plentiful rain and warm sun.
       (a)   (b)   (c) (d)

3. They are home to exotic creatures that live nowhere
    (a)   (b) (c)   (d)

   else on earth.

4. Rain forests also play an important role in the world's weather.
    (a)   (b) (c)   (d)

5. The highest part of the rain forest is called the canopy.
    (a)   (b) (c) (d)

6. The canopy contains the most colorful layer of rain-forest life.
    (a)   (b) (c)   (d)

7. There are brilliant flowers and fruits of every color.
    (a) (b)   (c) (d)

8. The most spectacular of the rain forest's creatures are its birds.
   (a) (b)   (c)   (d)

9. But insects win the grand prize — there are millions of insects in the rain forests.
    (a) (b)   (c) (d)

10. Some of the world's most valuable medicines come from the rain-forest plants.
     (a)   (b) (c)   (d)

11. Let's save the rain forests so that future generations can benefit from them.
    (a) (b)   (c) (d)

Date: _____

An **adjective** helps you imagine how something looks, feels, smells, sounds or tastes.

Write a list of adjectives on each bucket to fit the bucket's category.

words that
describe size

_____

_____

_____

words that describe
taste or smell

_____

_____

_____

words that
describe sounds

_____

_____

_____

words that describe how
something feels

_____

_____

_____

words that
describe weather

_____

_____

_____

words that
describe feelings

_____

_____

_____

Date: _____

*An **adjective** is a word that describes a noun. It helps you imagine how something feels, looks, smells, sounds or tastes. An **adjective** often tells what kind or how many. Look at the noun **arrow**, at the top of the triangle. Then read each line. The adjectives are underlined. Note how they help to tell more about the arrow.*

arrow
<u>red</u> arrow
<u>sleek</u> <u>red</u> arrow
<u>straight</u> <u>sleek</u> <u>red</u> arrow

Complete these triangles. Add adjectives on each line to describe the nouns.

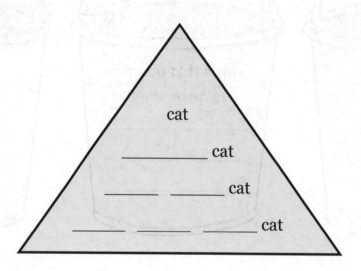

cat

_____ cat

_____ _____ cat

_____ _____ _____ cat

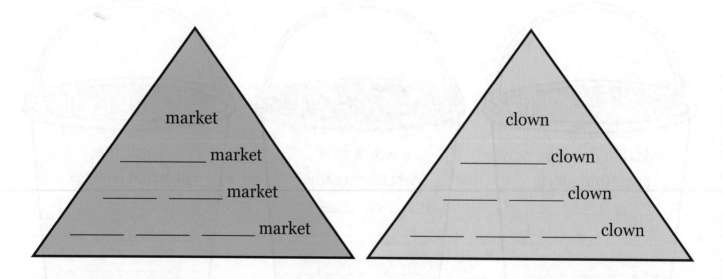

market

_____ market

_____ _____ market

_____ _____ _____ market

clown

_____ clown

_____ _____ clown

_____ _____ _____ clown

 Write a sentence using the noun and all the adjectives from one of the triangles you completed.

© 2013 Scholastic Education International (S) Pte Ltd ISBN 978-981-07-1369-0

Date: _____

Possessive adjectives *come before nouns and show ownership. Some possessive adjectives are:* **my, his, her, its, your, our** *and* **their.**

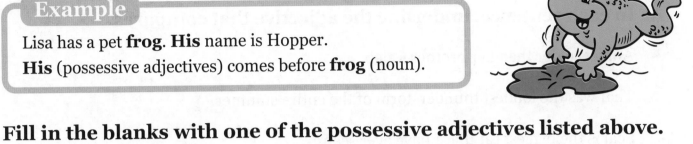

Example

Lisa has a pet **frog. His** name is Hopper.
His (possessive adjectives) comes before **frog** (noun).

Fill in the blanks with one of the possessive adjectives listed above.

1. The firemen showed _____ class how to climb a ladder.

2. Peter cleaned _____ room.

3. Kate loves to play soccer. _____ favorite position is goalie.

4. The students planned a surprise party for _____ teacher.

5. "Mrs Ruiz, please take _____ students through the museum."

6. We celebrated _____ team's win against the visitors.

7. "_____ dog just had puppies," said Karen.

8. The boy thanked _____ teacher for helping him with his French homework.

9. Bobby, Joel and Jack helped _____ coach put away the baseball equipment.

10. The spider spun _____ web near the door.

11. Julie came into the room and asked, "Why are _____ papers all over the floor?"

12. Why can't you put _____ things away neatly?

13. After Vernon saw the movie, he got into _____ car and drove away.

14. The girls said a few words and then put _____ coats on and went home.

15. _____ mom was so tired that we cooked dinner for her.

Comparative adjectives *compare two things by adding* **-er** *to the adjective or by using the word* **more**. **Superlative adjectives** *compare three or more things by adding* **-est** *or by using the word* **most**.

A. In each sentence, underline the adjective that compares.

1. Anna is older than her brother Caleb.

2. That was the loudest thunderstorm of the entire summer.

3. Seal is the biggest cat that I have ever seen.

4. Tim is quieter than Sarah.

5. The roof of the barn is higher than the top of the haystack.

6. The kitten's fur was softer than lamb's wool.

7. Sarah pointed to the brightest star in the sky.

8. What is the saddest moment in the story?

B. Underline the adjective in brackets ( ) that completes each sentence correctly. On the line write two or more than two to show how many things are being compared.

1. On the (hotter, hottest) day in July, we went swimming. _____

2. Today is (warmer, warmest) than last Tuesday. _____

3. Is winter (colder, coldest) on the prairie or by the sea? _____

4. This is the (taller, tallest) tree in the entire state. _____

5. Sarah's hair is (longer, longest) than Maggie's. _____

6. Of the three dogs, Nick was the (friendlier, friendliest). _____

7. Caleb's horse is (younger, youngest) than Anna's pony. _____

8. The new foal is the (livelier, liveliest) animal on the farm. _____

Fill in the letter of the answer that best completes each sentence.

1. This rock is _____ to climb than the other one.

   (a) hard   (b) harder   (c) hardest   (d) more harder

2. It has the _____ face of all the beginner's rocks in the area.

   (a) smooth   (b) smoother   (c) smoothest   (d) most smoothest

3. Rock climbing is _____ nowadays, thanks to modern gear.

   (a) safer   (b) more safer   (c) most safe   (d) safest

4. Climbers wear special shoes that have the _____ grip.

   (a) great   (b) greater   (c) greatest   (d) more greater

5. New climbers practice _____ than experienced ones to build confidence and skill.

   (a) often   (b) more often   (c) most often   (d) oftenest

6. They are told not to go _____ than their trainers tell them to.

   (a) farther   (b) more far   (c) farthest   (d) more farthest

7. Some cities have indoor climbing walls that are _____ than actual rocks.

   (a) difficult   (b) more difficulter   (c) difficulter   (d) more difficult

8. The _____ my local indoor climbing wall opens is 6:00 a.m.

   (a) early   (b) earlier   (c) most early   (d) earliest

Date: _____

 Adverbs can tell **when**, **where**, **how** *or* **how much**.

Answer each question using one or more of the adverbs from the Word Box. Complete the sentences.

Word Box

always
eagerly
loudly
rarely
slowly
occasionally
usually
very

1. When does it rain in the desert?

   It _____ rains in the desert.

2. How do most animals move in the heat?

   Most animals move _____

   _____.

3. How does a cactus grow?

   A cactus grows _____

   _____.

4. How do thirsty creatures drink?

   Thirsty creatures drink _____

   _____.

5. How often should you drink water when you are in the desert?

   When I am in the desert, I should _____

   _____.

Date: _____

A sentence needs two parts, a subject and a predicate, to express a complete thought. The **subject part** tells whom or what the sentence is about. The **predicate part** tells what the subject is or does.

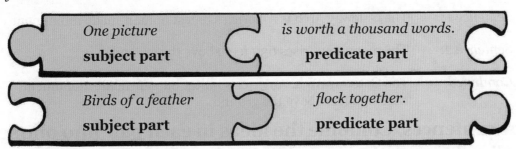

| One picture | is worth a thousand words. |
| **subject part** | **predicate part** |

| Birds of a feather | flock together. |
| **subject part** | **predicate part** |

A. Read the subject and predicate parts from some other famous sayings. Write S next to each subject part. Write P next to each predicate part.

1. _____ half a loaf
2. _____ catches the worm
3. _____ one good turn
4. _____ the early bird
5. _____ spoils the whole barrel
6. _____ must go on
7. _____ the show
8. _____ has a silver lining
9. _____ every cloud
10. _____ one rotten apple
11. _____ deserves another
12. _____ is better than none

B. Now combine the subject and predicate parts to create the famous sayings.

1. _____
2. _____
3. _____
4. _____
5. _____
6. _____

If two sentences share the same subject, information about the subject can be written as a phrase after the subject in the new sentence. Be sure to use commas to set apart the phrase from the rest of the sentence.

Sentence 1: The Gateway Arch is America's tallest human-made monument.

Sentence 2: The monument rises 630 feet above the ground.

Combined: The Gateway Arch, America's tallest human-made monument, rises 630 feet above the ground.

Read the sentences. Combine the ideas in each pair into one sentence by including information in a phrase after the subject in the sentence.

1. The Caspian Sea is the world's largest lake.
   The lake covers an area about the same size as Montana.

   _____

   _____

2. The Komodo dragon is a member of the monitor family.
   It can grow to a length of 10 feet.

   _____

   _____

3. Our closest star is the sun.
   Its temperature is estimated to be more than 27,000,000°F.

   _____

   _____

4. The Sahara is a desert in Africa.
   It is almost as large as China.

   _____

   _____

5. Snow White is a fairy-tale character.
   She has skin as white as snow and lips as red as blood.

   _____

   _____

© 2013 Scholastic Education International (S) Pte Ltd ISBN 978-981-07-1369-0

Date: _____

*Using the conjunction **and** shows you are joining ideas of the same kind.
Using the conjunction **but** shows the difference between two clauses.
Using the conjunction **or** shows a choice.*

Write the correct conjunction in the blank.

1. Mrs Goodwin gave us a choice of behaving _____ losing our recess.

2. Apples, oranges _____ grapes are on the table for a snack.

3. I cannot decide if I want to go to a movie _____ stay at home.

4. I know I have worked hard, _____ I wonder if my teacher has noticed.

5. Superman is very strong _____ he can fly.

6. Mary loves summer vacation, _____ she is always ready to get back to school.

7. Jada can eat a big lunch now _____ she can wait and eat a big dinner later.

8. Fred wants to be in the band and play tennis after school, _____ he cannot do both.

9. I like both Ted _____ Jim equally.

10. Did you want both chicken _____ fish for dinner?

11. I thought she said "three," _____ she really said "tree."

12. Polly wants to go, _____ I want to stay.

Date: _____

 When you write, you may want to show how the ideas in two simple sentences are related. You can combine the two sentences by using a comma and the conjunctions **and**, **but** *or* **or** *to show the connection.* **And** *shows a link between the ideas,* **but** *shows a contrast and* **or** *shows a choice. The new sentence is called a* **compound sentence**.

My sister wants to join a football team. My parents aren't so happy about it.
My sister wants to join a football team, but my parents aren't so happy about it.

Annie is determined. Her friends think she'd make a great place kicker.
Annie is determined, and her friends think she'd make a great place kicker.

Should Annie play football? Should she try something else?
Should Annie play football, or should she try something else?

Combine each pair of sentences. Use and, but or or to show the connection between the ideas and make a compound sentence.

1. My sister Annie has always participated in sports. Many say she's a natural athlete.

   _____

   _____

2. Soccer, basketball and softball are fun. She wanted a new challenge.

   _____

   _____

3. My sister talked to my brother and me. We were honest with her.

   _____

   _____

4. I told Annie to go for it. My brother told her to stick with soccer or basketball.

   _____

   _____

5. Will Dad convince her to try skiing? Will he suggest ice skating?

   _____

   _____

© 2013 Scholastic Education International (S) Pte Ltd ISBN 978-981-07-1369-0

Date: _____

Sentences can also be combined to make them more interesting. Key words can help put two sentences together.

Old: I will plan my garden. I am waiting for spring.

New: I will plan my garden while I am waiting for spring.

Write a new sentence using the key word in each flower.

1. Fill a cup with water. Add some flower seeds.

_____

2. This will soften the seeds. They are hard.

_____

3. Fill a cup with dirt. The seeds soak in water.

_____

4. Bury the seeds in the cup. The dirt covers them.

_____

5. Add water to the plant. Do not add too much.

_____

6. Set the cup in the sun. The plant will grow.

_____

Date: _____

Sometimes you can use words such as when, because, while *and* before *to combine two sentences with related ideas into one sentence with a main clause and a dependent clause. A* **clause** *is a group of words with a subject and a predicate. A* **dependent clause** *cannot stand alone. An* **independent clause** *can stand alone.*

Lee woke up late today. He realized he hadn't set the alarm last night.
<u>When Lee woke up late today,</u> <u>he realized he hadn't set his alarm last night.</u>

↑   ↑

This is a dependent clause.   *This is an independent clause.*

When the dependent clause comes before the main clause as in the above sentence, add a comma after the dependent clause. If the dependent clause follows the main clause, you do not need a comma. Here's an example.

Lee was upset. He was going to be late for school.
Lee was upset **because** he was going to be late for school.

Use the word inside the brackets ( ) to combine each pair of sentences into one.

1. I waited for my parents to get home. I watched a movie. (while)

   _____

2. My brother was in his room. He had homework to do. (because)

   _____

3. The movie was over. The power went out. (before)

   _____

4. This happens all the time. I wasn't concerned. (since)

   _____

5. I didn't mind the dark at first. I heard a scratching sound. (until)

   _____

6. I found my flashlight. I started to look around. (when)

   _____

7. I was checking the living room. I caught Alex trying to hide. (when)

   _____

Date: _____

 A sentence includes a subject and a verb. A sentence is more interesting when it also includes a part that tells where, when or why.

Add more information to each sentence by telling where, when or why. Write the complete new sentence.

1. Mom is taking us shopping.  Where?

_____

_____

2. The stores are closing. When?

_____

_____

3. We need to find a gift for Dad.  Why?

_____

_____

4. I will buy new jeans. Where?

_____

_____

5. We may eat lunch. When?

_____

_____

Date: _____

You know that you must use commas in a series of three or more items.
Max, Sam and Alex ordered burgers, fries and milkshakes for lunch.

Here are some additional rules you need to know about commas.
Use commas

— *to set off the name of the person or group you are addressing.*
Here's your order, boys.

— *after words like yes, no and well.*
Well, what do you want to do now?

— *before a conjunction that joins two sentences.*
The boys finished lunch, and then they went to a movie.

Read the sentences below. Decide which ones need commas and which ones do not. Use the symbol (,) to show where commas belong.

1. I'd like a bike a pair of in-line skates and a snowboard for my birthday.

2. Well my friend you can't always have what you want when you want it.

3. No but I can always hope!

4. My friends and I skate all year long and we snowboard during the winter.

5. I used to like skateboarding but now I prefer snowboarding and in-line skating.

6. What sports games or hobbies do you enjoy most Jody?

7. I learned to ski last year and now I'm taking ice-skating lessons.

8. Skiing ice skating and skateboarding are all fun things to do.

Review the four rules above for using commas. Then write an original sentence for each rule. Begin and end each sentence correctly. Remember to check your spelling.

9. _____

10. _____

11. _____

12. _____

© 2013 Scholastic Education International (S) Pte Ltd   ISBN 978-981-07-1369-0

Some stories may include dialogue, or the exact words of story characters. Dialogue lets readers know something about the characters, plot, setting and problem or conflict in a story. Use quotation marks around a speaker's exact words and commas to set off quotations. Remember to put periods, question marks, exclamation points and commas inside the quotation marks.

"Get away from my bowl!" yelled Little Miss Muffet when she saw the approaching spider.

"Please don't get so excited," replied the startled spider. "I just wanted a little taste. I've never tried curds and whey before."

Use your imagination to complete the dialogue between the fairy tale or nursery rhyme characters. Include quotation marks and commas where they belong and the correct end punctuation.

1. When Baby Bear saw the strange girl asleep in his bed, he asked his parents,

   _____

   His mother replied, _____

2. Humpty Dumpty was sitting on the wall when he suddenly fell off. On the way

   down he shouted, _____

   Two of the king's men approached. One whispered nervously to the other,

   _____

3. When Jack realized he was about to fall down the hill with a pail of water, he yelled,

   _____

   cried Jill, as she went tumbling down the hill after Jack.

4. The wolf knocked on the door of her grandmother's house. When there was no answer,

   the wolf bellowed, _____

   Knowing that it was the wolf, Little Red Riding Hood said, _____

   _____

Date: _____

*You can compare two things that are not alike in order to give your readers a clearer and more colorful picture. When you use **like** or **as** to make a comparison, it is called a **simile**.*

Max is as slow as molasses when he doesn't want to do something.

My sister leaped over the puddles like a frog to avoid getting her shoes wet.

The angry man erupted like a volcano.

Complete the similes with a suitable word.

1. Without her glasses, Mrs Wong is as _____ as a bat.

2. Alice has a pretty dress. It's as _____ as a rainbow.

3. The boys are as _____ as a herd of elephants. They will wake the baby.

4. Have you been eating well? You are as _____ as a toothpick!

5. Dr Samy is so smart, he is like a wise _____.

6. You need to bring a flashlight because it is as dark as _____ in the cave.

7. Don't worry about Tom in the water. He swims like a _____.

8. The bus was so crowded that we were squashed like _____ in a can.

*When you make a comparison without like or as, it is called a **metaphor**. You compare things directly, saying the subject is something else.*

As soon as the teacher left the room, it turned into <u>a fish market</u>. (a noisy place)

Mrs Terry is <u>such an angel</u>. She does so much to help her neighbors. (very kind)

Jenny and I were <u>all ears</u> as we listened to the latest gossip. (very attentive)

What do these metaphors mean? Circle the word(s) that describe(s) the meaning.

1. Those basketball players are **giants**. How can we beat them?

   small   tall   large   kind

2. John is **such a mule** that you will not be able to make him change his mind.

   hardworking   stubborn   clever   angry

3. Mr Krishnan is **a rock** in his family. They know they can count on him.

   strong   reliable   fat   hard

4. This idea is **such a gem**! We are so glad you shared it with us.

   sensible   brilliant   precious   new

5. This town is **a hive of activity** whenever the famous actor visits.

   crowded   unfriendly   busy   quiet

Date: _____

 If your topic is too broad, it will be hard for you to treat it well. Examine this example of narrowing a topic:

Broad topic: Movies

Narrow topic: Adventure movies

Narrower topic: Movies about adventures in space

Complete the chart by narrowing the given topics.

	Broad	Narrow	Narrower
1.	team sports	indoor team sports	
2.	foods	desserts	
3.	ocean creatures	sharks	
4.	instruments		playing the harp
5.	South America	jungles of South America	
6.	lakes	The Great Lakes	
7.	careers	careers in medicine	
8.	transportation	one-person vehicles	
9.	planets		Is there life on Mars?
10.	dinosaurs	meat-eating dinosaurs	

A **paragraph** is a group of sentences that tells about one main idea. The **topic sentence** tells the main idea and is usually the first sentence. **Supporting sentences** tell more about the main idea. The **closing sentence** of a paragraph often retells the main idea in a different way. Here are the parts for one paragraph.

Paragraph title:	Starting Over
Topic sentence:	Today started off badly and only got worse.
Supporting sentences:	1. Everyone in my family woke up late this morning.
	2. I had only 15 minutes to get ready and catch the bus.
	3. I dressed as fast as I could, grabbed an apple and my backpack, and raced to get to the bus stop on time.
	4. Fortunately, I just made it.
	5. Unfortunately, when I was on the bus, several kids pointed out that I had on two different shoes.
Closing sentence:	At that moment, I wanted to start the day over.

When you write a paragraph, remember these rules:

- **Indent** *the first line to let readers know that you are beginning a paragraph.*
- **Capitalize** *the first word of each sentence.*
- **Punctuate** *each sentence correctly (? ! . ,).*

Use all the information and rules above to write the paragraph.

_____

Paragraph Title

_____

_____

_____

_____

_____

_____

Every paragraph has a topic sentence that tells the main idea of the paragraph, or what it is about. It usually answers several of these questions:

Who? What? Where? When? Why? How?

Here are some examples.

The doe and her fawn faced many dangers in the forest.

We were amazed by our guest's rude behavior.

Baking bread from scratch is really not so difficult, or so I thought.

Did these topic sentences grab your attention? A good topic sentence should.

Here are some topics. Write a topic sentence for each one.

1. convincing someone to try octopus soup

   _____

2. an important person in your life

   _____

3. an embarrassing moment

   _____

4. the importance of a country's National Day

   _____

5. lunchtime at the school cafeteria

   _____

Now list some topics of your own. Then write a topic sentence for each one.

		Topic 1		Topic 2
Topic sentence 1				
Topic sentence 2				

Read each topic sentence. Then read the three sentences that follow it. Fill in the letter next to the sentence that best supports the topic sentence.

1. **Topic sentence:** The pyramids are the stone tombs of Egypt's kings — the Pharaohs.

   (a) The dry desert heat helped to keep the Pharaoh's body from rotting.

   (b) They have stood for thousands of years, filled with many hidden secrets.

   (c) The Sphinx stands in front of all the pyramids in Giza.

2. **Topic sentence:** The Grand Canyon is among the Earth's greatest geological spectacles.

   (a) The Grand Canyon National Park was first designated a forest reserve in 1893.

   (b) Hunting was allowed there until it became a game reserve in 1906.

   (c) The information it reveals about the Earth's history is invaluable.

3. **Topic sentence:** Mt Waaileale in Hawaii is the wettest place on Earth!

   (a) It is located on the small island of Kauai.

   (b) This soggy spot gets about 460 inches of rain every year.

   (c) In the Hawaiian language, the word *waialeale* means "rippling water."

4. **Topic sentence:** Mount Fuji in Japan is known to be a "shy" mountain.

   (a) It constantly hides behind haze or cloud.

   (b) Much of the western sky in Tokyo is taken up by a view of Mount Fuji.

   (c) Climbing Mount Fuji is an experience of a lifetime.

5. **Topic sentence:** The Taj Mahal is a beautiful monument in India.

   (a) It was built by Emperor Shah Jahan for his dear wife, Mumtaz Mahal.

   (b) Built of white marble, its beauty is stunning at dawn and sunset.

   (c) Taj Mahal was built over a period of 22 years, employing 20,000 workers.

*There are many kinds of paragraphs. When you write a **compare-and-contrast paragraph**, you compare by telling how things are similar and contrast by telling how things are different. You can use a Venn diagram to help organize your ideas.*

Trumpet   **Both**   **Violin**

- brass
- has a mouthpiece
- has three valves

- are played in orchestras
- musical instruments
- take practice

- wood
- four strings
- played with a bow

Complete the paragraph using details to compare and contrast the trumpet and violin. Remember to capitalize and punctuate correctly.

Trumpet Versus Violin

The trumpet and the violin are both musical instruments that are _____

_____. However, there are some

important differences. The trumpet _____

_____

_____

_____

On the other hand, the violin _____

_____

_____

_____

Both instruments _____

_____

© 2013 Scholastic Education International (S) Pte Ltd   ISBN 978-981-07-1369-0

Date: _____

*A **descriptive paragraph** creates a vivid image or picture for readers. By choosing just the right adjectives, you can reveal how something looks, sounds, smells, tastes and feels. Compare the sentences from two different paragraphs. Which one creates a more vivid picture?*

The pizza with sausage and onions tasted so good.

The smooth, sweet sauce and bubbly mozzarella topped with bite-sized chunks of extra hot sausage and thin slivers of sweet onion on a perfectly baked, thin crust delighted my taste buds.

Cut out a picture of something interesting and paste it in the box. Then brainstorm a list of adjectives and descriptive phrases to tell about it.

_____ _____

_____ _____

_____ _____

_____ _____

_____ _____

_____ _____

Now, write a paragraph about the picture. Begin your paragraph with a topic sentence that will grab attention. Add supporting sentences that include the adjectives and descriptive phrases listed to create a vivid picture.

_____

_____

_____

_____

_____

Date: _____

 A **persuasive paragraph** *gives your opinion and tries to convince the reader to agree. Its supporting ideas are reasons that back up your opinion.*

Topic sentence   *Reason 2*

Reason 1 → Our family should have a dog for three reasons. First, pets teach responsibility. If we get a dog, I will feed him and take him for walks after school. The second reason for having a pet is that he would make a good companion for me when everyone else is busy. I won't drive Dad crazy by always asking him to play catch with me. The third reason we need a dog is for safety. He would warn us of danger and keep our house safe. For all of these reasons, I'm sure you'll agree that we should jump in the car and head toward the adoption agency right away. I don't know how we have made it this long without a dog! *← Closing sentence*

Reason 3 ——

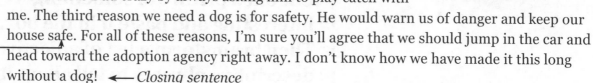

Plan and write a persuasive paragraph asking your parents for something (such as a family trip, expensive new shoes or a camera).

1. Choose a topic: _____

2. Write a topic sentence: _____

   _____

3. Brainstorm three supporting reasons:

   Reason 1 _____

   Reason 2 _____

   Reason 3 _____

4. Write a closing sentence: _____

   _____

Date: _____

When you keep a journal, you can record the facts and details about events that happen in your life and your feelings or opinions about them. Your journal entries can be a valuable resource when you are looking for writing ideas.

3/9 We had to take Fuzzer to his new home today. Our new landlord said he could not stay with us at our apartment anymore. I know Fuzzer will be much happier at the farm where he can run and play, but I still felt so sad. I tried not to cry, but I could not help it. Fuzzer has been part of our family for nine years. We grew up together. I will miss him very much!

3/15 I had to go to my sister's dance recital at the Palace Theater last night. She performed in three numbers. At first I didn't want to go because I thought it would be boring, but it wasn't. I actually felt really proud of my sister! She was fantastic. I guess I really should tell her.

Think about the events that have happened in your life over the last several days. Did anything of special importance happen that affected you? Record the facts, details and your feelings or opinions about two events on the journal page below. Write the date for each entry.

_____/ _____/ _____

_____

_____

_____

_____

_____/ _____/ _____

_____

_____

_____

Each sentence below contains one kind of error — or no error at all. Choose the best answer.

1. So, are you sure you know all your times tables.

- (a) capitalization error
- (b) spelling error
- (c) punctuation error
- (d) no error

2. Which is the top number in a fraction — the numerator or the denominator?

- (a) capitalization error
- (b) spelling error
- (c) punctuation error
- (d) no error

3. Geometry, the study of lines angles and shapes is my favorite topic in math.

- (a) capitalization error
- (b) spelling error
- (c) punctuation error
- (d) no error

4. Our math teacher told us why the equil sign is made of two lines.

- (a) capitalization error
- (b) spelling error
- (c) punctuation error
- (d) no error

5. Our Principal says that he is more than two yards tall.

- (a) capitalization error
- (b) spelling error
- (c) punctuation error
- (d) no error

6. My ruler is marked in inches along one edge and in centimeters along the other.

- (a) capitalization error
- (b) spelling error
- (c) punctuation error
- (d) no error

Date: _____

Find and mark the twelve errors in the following. They may be spelling, punctuation, capitalization or grammar errors.

Diary of a Dog

by Louie the Dog

Dear Diary,

Today I get up. I did some scrathing because my neck itched. Then I slept. Then I did some sniffing around. Then I slept. Then I barked at the maillman. After that, I took a nap until dinnertime. for dinner, I had pellets in a dish. then I went back to sleep.

Yours truly, Louie

Dear Diary,

Today I saw a small white cats out in the yard. This really made me mad! So I barked a lot. I felt better afterwards. Do you know what I ate for dinner. I ate pellets! I washed it all down with a big slirp of water.

Then I go back to sleep.

Yours truly, Louie

Dear Diary,

I just felt like barking todae. So I barked and barked. Then I eaten pellets and went to sleep.

Yours truly, Louie

Dear Diary,

That mailman comes every day. I'm getting tired of banking at him. But I did it anyway. Also, I took a walk. Tomorrow I'll catch up on my sleeping.

Yours truly, Louie

Have you ever accidentally left out words when you write? Whenever you write, it is always a good idea to proofread for words that may be missing. Here is an example of what to do when you want to add a missing word as you proofread.

         e-mail
I got an ∧ from my friend last night.

   met
We ∧ last summer when my family was in Japan.

Read the passage below about school in Japan. Twenty words are missing. Figure out what they are and add them to the sentences. Use the ∧ symbol to show where each missing word belongs. Then write each missing word above the sentence. (Hint: Every sentence has at least one missing word.)

How would like to go to school on Saturdays? If you lived in the of Japan, that's just where you'd be each Saturday morning. I have a who lives in Japan. Yuichi explained that attend classes five and one-half a week. I was also surprised to that the Japanese school is one of the longest in the world. It's over 240 days. The year begins in the of April. While some countries have over two months off each, students in Japan get their in late July and August. School then again in fall and ends in March. The people of believe that a good is very important. Children are required to attend school from the age of six to the of fifteen. They have elementary and middle. Then most go on to school for another three years. Yuichi says that students work very because the standards are so high. He and some of his friends even extra classes after school. They all want to get into a good someday.

Do you sometimes run together several ideas into one long, run-on sentence?

According to my grandma, it is a good idea to eat chicken soup when you have a cold and believe it or not, scientists agree with her the protein in the soup fights the stuffiness by thinning out the lining of your sinuses.

You can easily fix a run-on sentence by rewriting each complete idea as a separate sentence. Begin each sentence with a capital letter and end it with the correct punctuation mark.

According to my grandma, it is a good idea to eat chicken soup when you have a cold. Believe it or not, scientists agree with her! The protein in the soup fights the stuffiness by thinning out the lining of your sinuses.

Rewrite each run-on sentence correctly.

1. Did you know that carrots really are good for your eyes there is a vitamin in this crunchy orange root called beta-carotene that helps lower the risk of eye disease and so the next time you find carrot sticks in your lunch don't trade them or toss them away munch away in good health instead?

   _____

   _____

   _____

   _____

2. Do you like potato chips, cookies, cake and ice-cream if you're like me, you probably do and I'm sure you also know that these wonderful tasty treats are considered to be junk food and it is a good idea to eat small amounts of food with a lot of fat, oil, sugar and salt?

   _____

   _____

   _____

   _____

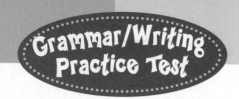
Fill in the bubble next to the correct answer.

1. Which common noun names the group that contains: New York, Seoul, Hong Kong, Paris?

- **A** provinces
- **B** countries
- **C** states
- **D** cities

2. Which word in the following sentence is a possessive pronoun?

The students planned a surprise party for their teacher.

- **A** The
- **B** students
- **C** surprise
- **D** their

3. Which sentence has NO punctuation mistake?

- **A** The main ingredients are flour, butter, eggs, and milk.
- **B** The frame's he makes are made of natural twigs.
- **C** The kittens were born on January 9 2012.
- **D** How late will the post office remain open tonight.

Fill in the bubble next to the correct answer.

4. Which word is the correct noun that matches the meaning of the underlined pronoun in the following sentence?

> I read a book about the plants and animals that live in the rain forest. <u>Its</u> author was a well-known scientist.

○ **A**   the plants'

○ **B**   the animals'

○ **C**   the book's

○ **D**   the rain forest's

5. Which sentence best supports the topic sentence "Adopting a Pet?"

○ **A**   We won a huge stuffed animal at the fair.

○ **B**   He went straight to the food.

○ **C**   It's always best to know the animal's previous owner.

○ **D**   The basket can safely hold three or four puppies.

6. Which word best completes the following sentence?

> It was the annual barbecue, _____ our entire family gathers for a picnic.

○ **A**   with

○ **B**   although

○ **C**   because

○ **D**   when

Fill in the bubble next to the correct answer.

7. Which word means the opposite of the underlined word in the following sentence?
The mayor's <u>loyal</u> aide takes care of every assignment.

○ **A**   unfaithful

○ **B**   tardy

○ **C**   part-time

○ **D**   reliable

8. Which word would you use to combine the following short sentences?
The coach blew her whistle. The game stopped.

○ **A**   because

○ **B**   for

○ **C**   and

○ **D**   since

9. Write the correct form of the verb in brackets ( ) to complete the following sentence.
Yesterday I (to feed) the cat tuna.

○ **A**   feed

○ **B**   feeds

○ **C**   fed

○ **D**   will feed

Fill in the bubble next to the correct answer.

10. Look at the underlined noun in the following sentence and tell whether it names a person, place, thing or idea.

Scientists look at small objects under a <u>microscope</u>.

○ **A**   person

○ **B**   place

○ **C**   thing

○ **D**   idea

11. Read the following sentence. Which linking verb correctly completes the sentence?

From 1860 to 1945, Denver _____ a mining and agricultural community.

○ **A**   were

○ **B**   was

○ **C**   is

○ **D**   will be

12. Read the following sentence. Does it contain any error? If so, what kind of error does it contain?

Farmer John made a Scarecrow to frighten the crows away from his garden.

○ **A**   capitalization error

○ **B**   spelling error

○ **C**   punctuation error

○ **D**   no error

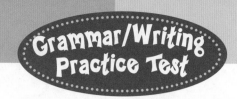

Fill in the bubble next to the correct answer.

13. Siva wants to know the meaning of the word **inception**. It will be on the dictionary page that has which guide words?

- ○ **A**   increase/incubate
- ○ **B**   incessant/incorporate
- ○ **C**   incantation/income
- ○ **D**   incorporate/incur

14. Which of the following words is a noun?

- ○ **A**   beautiful
- ○ **B**   quickly
- ○ **C**   friendliest
- ○ **D**   machine

15. Which of these is a run-on sentence?

- ○ **A**   More than 40 fish produce electricity the most dangerous is the electric eel.
- ○ **B**   The electric eel gives off electric signals to "see" in the dark where it lives.
- ○ **C**   Once the electric eel locates its prey, it fills the water with an electric shock.
- ○ **D**   The electric charge is so strong it could knock over a full-grown horse!

Answer Key

Spelling

Page 6

A. short -a: dragon, gather, handle; ai: plains, raise, wait; a_e: brave, mistake, became; ay: today, maybe, holiday

B. mistake, raise, holiday, became

Page 7

A. holiday, wait, brave, dragon, gather, maybe

B. 1. mistake   2. raise   3. gather   4. became   5. today   6. plains   7. handle;   FIREBALL

Page 8

A. short -e: member, next, check, enter; ea: scream, reason, reach, team; ee: cheek, freeze, asleep, between

B. scream, cheek, freeze, check

Page 9

A. 1. enter   2. scream   3. freeze   4. team   5. member   6. asleep

B. Across: scream, member, cheek; Backward: check, team, asleep; Down: between, reach, enter; Diagonally: next, reason, freeze

C. 7. big; soccer
   8. chess; tennis
   9. ball; basketball

Page 10

A. short -i: winter, middle, kitchen, children; i_e: surprise, polite, while, strike; igh: bright, frighten, tight, slight

B. surprise, middle, polite, while, strike

Page 11

A. 1. polite   2. strike   3. frighten   4. kitchen   5. children   6. winter

B. 7. middle   8. bright   9. slight   10. surprise   11. tight   12. while   13. kitchen   14. strike   15. polite

C. 16. igloo   17. sleigh   18. icicle

Page 12

A. short -o: rocket, monster, holler, bottle; o_e: alone, globe, whole, suppose; ow: pillow, below, window; short -o and ow: follow

B. pillow, follow, holler, bottle, suppose

Page 13

A. pillow, rocket, holler, window, whole, bottle, suppose

B. 1. globe   2. below   3. whole   4. holler   5. pillow   6. bottle   7. suppose   8. follow   9. rocket   10. window 11. alone   12. monster

C. 1. clothes   2. tomorrow   3. trouble

Page 14

A. short -u: until, number, sudden; long -u: super, ruler, duty; oo: loose, shampoo, caboose; ou: coupon, group, soup

B. coupon, ruler, shampoo, soup, caboose, number, group, duty

Page 15

A. 1. coupon   2. ruler   3. group   4. loose   5. shampoo   6. until; CEREAL

B. 7. caboose, number
   8. coupon, loose   9. soup, super;

C. supermarket, groceries, teaspoon

Page 16

A. -er: swimmer, safer, freezer; -est: wisest, biggest, whitest; -ed: hoped, clapped, stopped; -ing: shopping, getting, coming

B. wisest, hoped, safer, freezer, whitest

Page 17

A. 1. biggest; double the final consonant
   2. hoped; drop the silent e
   3. coming; drop the silent e
   4. getting; double the final consonant
   5. whitest; drop the silent e
   6. wisest; drop the silent e

B. 1. coming   2. shopping
   3. clapped   4. stopped
   5. swimmer   6. freezer
   7. hoped   8. safer;
   COLD MEDAL

Page 18

changes -f to -ves: loaves, wolves, calves, halves, thieves, scarves, knives, shelves; changes -oo- to -ee-: geese, teeth; unusual plural forms: oxen, children, cacti, mice, women

Page 19

A. 1. calves   2. geese   3. halves   4. teeth   5. shelves   6. cacti   7. oxen   8. knives   9. thieves   10. scarves 11. women   12. mice   13. loaves 14. children 15. wolves   16. geckos

B. Reptiles, vertebrates, Alligators, tortoises, predators

Page 20

A. Review ideas.

B. Review choices.

Page 21

A. 1. these   2. done   3. favorite   4. friend   5. before   6. always   7. their   8. people   9. thought   10-12. does, done, been 13. always   14. their/these   15. favorite   16. other   17. people   18. friend

C. 19. animal; mammal

20. kind; breed

21. dogs; canines

Page 22

A. one vowel: forty, truly; two vowels: once, meant, young, island, toward, answer, often; three vowels: another, against, beauty, calendar, machine, cousin

Page 23

A. 1. island 2. cousin 3. forty

4. machine 5. beauty 6. calendar;

B. Once upon a time there was a young boy who would not study. He meant to study, but he always forgot. Thus, he would often need to guess an answer because he truly did not know it. While walking toward his house after school, he decided to lean against a tree. He watched a squirrel nibble on a nut. Another squirrel scampered up the tree. the squirrels were so fascinating the boy decided to learn about them. That night he discovered how interesting it is to study.

C. 7. sculpture   8. landscape

9. masterpiece 10. artistic

11. portrait   12. Mona Lisa

Pages 24–27

1. B   2. C   3. D   4. D

5. C   6. C   7. B   8. A

9. C   10. D   11. D   12. C

Grammar and Writing

Page 29

A. 1. Q   2. S   3. S   4. Q

5. Q   6. S   7. S   8. Q

B. 1. How did the ant carry the crumb?

2. She carried it herself.

3. The rooster was very busy.

Page 30

A. 1. E   2. C   3. C   4. E

5. E   6. C   7. E   8. C

B. Review sentences.

Page 31

1. c   2. b   3. d   4. b

5. b   6. d   7. b   8. a

9. c   10. b   11. b   12. b

Page 32

2-10. Review the chosen proper nouns.

12. character   13. singer

14. car   15. book/movie

16. city   17. author

18. month   19. day of the week

20. national leader

Page 33

1. an   2. a   3. a   4. An

5. an   6. an   7. a   8. a

9. a   10. a   11. a   12. a

13. An   14. a   15. an

Page 34

1. it   2. me   3. You

4. I   5. him   6. us

7. them   8. her, she   9. we, them

10. it   11. you   12. us

Page 35

A. 1. We, S   2. us, O   3. You, S

4. I, S   5. it, O   6. her, O

7. them, O   8. She, S

B. 1. They sent a postcard to us.

2. It was addressed to him.

C. 1-2. Review sentences.

Page 36

1. c   2. a   3. b   4. c

5. a   6. d

Page 37

A. 1. out pictures of mountains, rivers and lakes; out, of

2. on the walls; on/of his room; of

3. on a camping trip; on

4. in a backpack and knapsack; in

5. from his father's mug; from

6. in the mountains; for hours; in, for

7. at the Lost Lake; at

8. on their journey; on

9. at a quiet place; for the night; at, for

10. in a tent; in

11. from the wind and rain; from

12. on their camping trip; on

B. Review sentences.

Page 28

1. d   2. b   3. a   4. a

5. c   6. b   7. b   8. a

9. c   10. c

Page 39

1. c   2. b   3. a   4. d

5. c   6. a   7. b   8. b

Page 40

1. c   2. c   3. a   4. a

5. a   6. b   7. a   8. b

9. b   10. a   11. d

Pages 41–42

Review adjectives.

Page 43

Possible answers:

1. our   2. his   3. Her

4. their   5. your   6. our

7. Our or My 8. his   9. their

10. its   11. my or your 12. your

13. his   14. their   15. Our

Page 44

A. 1. older 2. loudest 3. biggest
  4. quieter 5. higher 6. softer
  7. brightest 8. saddest

B. 1. hottest, more than two
  2. warmer, two
  3. colder, two
  4. tallest, more than two
  5. longer, two
  6. friendliest, more than two
  7. younger, two
  8. liveliest, more than two

Page 45

1. b 2. c 3. a 4. c
5. b 6. a 7. d 8. d

Page 46

1. (very) rarely
2. (very) slowly in the desert
3. (very) slowly
4. (very) eagerly
5. always drink water

Page 47

A. 1. S 2. P 3. S 4. S
  5. P 6. P 7. S 8. P
  9. S 10. S 11. P 12. P

B. 1. Half a loaf is better than none.
  2. One good turn deserves
    another.
  3. One rotten apple spoils the
    whole barrel.
  4. The show must go on.
  5. Every cloud has a silver lining.
  6. The early bird catches
    the worm.

Page 48

1. The Caspian Sea, the world's
  largest lake, covers an area about
  the same size as Montana.

2. The Komodo dragon, a member
  of the monitor family, can grow
  to a length of 10 feet.

3. The temperature of our closest
  star, the sun, is estimated to be
  more than 27,000,000°F.

4. The Sahara, a desert in Africa, is
  almost as large as China.

5. Snow White, a fairy-tale
  character, has skin as white as
  snow and lips as red as blood.

Page 49

1. or 2. and 3. or 4. but
5. and 6. but 7. or 8. but
9. and 10. and 11. but 12. but

Page 50

1. My sister Annie has always
  participated in sports, and many
  say she's a natural athlete.

2. Soccer, basketball and softball
  are fun, but she wanted a new
  challenge.

3. My sister talked to my brother and
  me, and we were honest with her.

4. I told Annie to go for it, but my
  brother told her to stick with
  soccer or basketball.

5. Will Dad convince her to try
  skiing, or will her suggest ice
  skating?

Page 51

1. Fill a cup with water and add
  some flower seeds.

2. This will soften the seeds because
  they are hard.

3. Fill a cup with dirt while the
  seeds soak in water.

4. Bury the seeds in the cup until
  the dirt covers them.

5. Add water to the plant, but do not
  add too much.

6. Set the cup in the sun so the plant
  will grow.

Page 52

Possible sentences:

1. I watched a movie while I waited
  for my parents to get home.

2. My brother was in his room
  because he had homework
  to do.

3. The power went out before the
  movie was over.

4. I wasn't concerned since this
  happens all the time.

5. I didn't mind the dark at first
  until I heard a scratching sound.

6. I started to look around when
  I found my flashlight.

7. I was checking the living room
  when I caught Alex trying to hide.

Page 53

Review sentences.

Page 54

1. I'd like a bike, a pair of in-line
  skates and a snowboard for my
  birthday.

2. Well, my friend, you can't always
  have what you want when you
  want it.

3. No, but I can always hope!

4. My friends and I skate all year
  long, and we snowboard during
  the winter.

5. I used to like skateboarding, but
  now I prefer snowboarding and
  in-line skating.

6. What sports, games or hobbies do
  you enjoy most, Jody?

7. I learned to ski last year, and now I'm taking ice-skating lessons.

8. Skiing, ice skating and skateboarding are all fun things to do.

9–12. Check that directions have been followed.

Page 55
Check that directions have been followed.

Page 56
1. blind 2. colorful 3. noisy
4. thin 5. owl 6. night
7. fish 8. sardines

Page 57
1. tall, large 2. stubborn
3. strong, reliable
4. brilliant, precious
5. crowded, busy

Page 58
Answers will vary.

Pages 59–60
Check that directions have been followed.

Page 61
1. b 2. c 3. b
4. a 5. b

Page 62
The trumpet and the violin are both musical instruments that are played in orchestras. However, there are some important differences. The trumpet is a brass instrument. It has a mouthpiece and has three valves. On the other hand, the violin is a wood instrument. It has four strings and is played with a bow. Both instruments take practice to play.

Page 63
Check that directions have been followed.

Page 64
Review paragraph.

Page 65
Check that directions have been followed.

Page 66
1. c 2. d 3. c
4. b 5. a 6. b

Page 67
got; scratching; mailman; For; Then; cat; dinner?; slurp; went; today; ate; barking

Page 68
How would you like to go to school on Saturdays? If you lived in the country of Japan, that's just where you'd be each Saturday morning. I have a friend who lives in Japan. Yuichi explained that students attend classes five and one-half days a week. I was also surprised to learn that the Japanese school year is one of the longest in the world. It's over 240 days long. The year begins in the month of April. While some countries have over two months off each year, students in Japan get their vacation in late July and August. School then starts again in fall and ends in March. The people of Japan believe that a good education is very important. Children are required to attend school from the age of six to the age of fifteen. They have elementary and middle school. Then most go on to high school for another three years. Yuichi says that students work very hard because the standards are so high. He and some of his friends even attend extra classes after school. They all want to get into a good college someday.

Page 69
1. Did you know that carrots really are good for your eyes? There is a vitamin in this crunchy orange root called beta-carotene that helps lower the risk of eye disease. So the next time you find carrot sticks in your lunch, don't trade them or toss them away. Munch away in good health instead!

2. Do you like potato chips, cookies, cake and ice-cream? If you're like me, you probably do. I'm sure you also know that these wonderful tasty treats are considered to be junk food. It is a good idea to eat small amounts of food with a lot of fat, oil, sugar and salt.

Pages 70–75
1. D 2. D 3. A 4. C
5. C 6. D 7. A 8. C
9. C 10. C 11. B 12. A
13. C 14. D 15. A

© 2013 Scholastic Education International (S) Pte Ltd ISBN 978-981-07-1369-0